To: Sheah

Secret Santa
'19

From: Aysha ♥

An Hachette UK Company
www.hachette.co.uk

First published in Great Britain in 2018 by Hamlyn,
a division of Octopus Publishing Group Ltd
Carmelite House, 50 Victoria Embankment, London EC4Y 0DZ
www.octopusbooks.co.uk

ISBN 978-0-7537-3315-8

A CIP catalogue record for this book is available from the British Library

Printed and bound in China

10 9 8 7 6 5 4 3 2 1

Publisher: Lucy Pessell
Designer: Lisa Layton
Editor: Sarah Vaughan
Production Manager: Caroline Alberti
Cover and interior motifs created by: AFY Studio, Alexander Skowalsky,
Rflor, Mister Pixel, A.Varghese. All from *The Noun Project*.

YOU
HAVE
THE POWER

AFFIRMATIONS
TO CHANGE YOUR LIFE

hamlyn

I AM
LOVED

MY LIFE
IS JUST
BEGINNING

I CAN
AND
I WILL

I
AM
ENOUGH

I WELCOME MIRACLES INTO MY LIFE

I AM
STRONG

I
AM
WORTHY
OF
LOVE

I HONOUR MYSELF IN EVERY DECISION I MAKE

I AM
PROUD
TO BE ME

I CAN
DO ALL
THINGS

I'M IN THE RIGHT PLACE, DOING THE RIGHT THING AT THE RIGHT TIME

I AM NOT ASHAMED OF WHO I AM OR WHERE I AM FROM

I
SHINE
BRIGHT

TODAY
IS A
NEW
DAY

I

AM

BEAUTIFUL

GREAT THINGS ARE AHEAD OF ME

I

BELIEVE

IN ME

TIME IS MY HEALER OF ALL THINGS

POSITIVE THOUGHTS BECOME POSITIVE THINGS

MY FUTURE IS MY OWN

I RUN TOWARDS THE CHALLENGES AHEAD OF ME WITH CONFIDENCE

I CAN DO THIS

I TRUST MYSELF

I DON'T SWEAT THE SMALL STUFF

FAILURE IS JUST MY OPPORTUNITY TO BEGIN AGAIN

TODAY IS A GIFT

I REJECT CYNICISM. I ACCEPT HOPE

THERE ARE TALENTS IN ME I AM YET TO SEE

I HAVE
A
PURPOSE

I
CHOOSE
HAPPINESS

I LEARN FROM MY MISTAKES. THEY DO NOT DEFEAT ME

THE UNIVERSE IS FOR ME, NOT AGAINST ME

I
AM
FREE

I HAVE THE POWER TO MAKE MY DREAMS COME TRUE

I AM
BRIMMING
WITH
ENOUGH
ENERGY
TO FACE
ANYTHING

I AM
MY OWN
SUPERHERO

I AM
HEALTHY

MY STRENGTHS OUTWEIGH MY WEAKNESSES

EACH DAY, I TRIUMPH

I
AM
BLESSED

I
ACCEPT
THE
BEST

MY VISION IS FULL OF HOPE AND EXPECTATION

I'M MEANT TO BE ME

PEACE INVADES EVERY PART OF MY MIND, BODY AND SOUL

I WILL
KEEP
GOING

WORRY
HAS NO
PLACE
IN ME

WHEN ONE DOOR CLOSES, ANOTHER OPENS

I
AM
UNSTOPPABLE

MY MIND IS FOCUSED

I WILL NOT COMPARE MYSELF TO OTHERS

I
CHOOSE
HAPPINESS

LOVE FLOWS FROM ME

I AM HAPPY IN MY OWN SKIN

I CAN
BE KIND
TO ME

I DESERVE
TRUE AND CARING
RELATIONSHIPS

THE GOODNESS I GIVE TO THE WORLD WILL COME BACK TO ME

MY
LIFE IS
WORTH
IT

I AM THE CHANGE I WANT TO SEE IN THE WORLD

MY LIFE

LIFE

IS A

CELEBRATION

I
LET GO
OF
NEGATIVITY

I

AM

WHOLE

I AM
DESTINED
FOR JOY

I
CAN
OVERCOME
MY
FEARS

SUCCESS FOLLOWS ME

WHEREVER I TURN, I PROSPER

I LET GO
OF WHAT
I CAN'T
CONTROL

EACH DAY
I TAKE THE
CHANCE TO
LEARN AND
TO GROW

I
RADIATE
LIGHT
AND
LIFE

THE
ONLY WAY
FOR ME
IS UP

I AM
CALM
AND
MINDFUL

I AM
THANKFUL
FOR EACH DAY

MY BEST SOURCE OF MOTIVATION IS ME

I
ATTRACT
HAPPINESS
INTO
MY
LIFE

MY STORY IS FULL OF HAPPY ENDINGS

I WALK THIS WORLD WITH GRACE

I HAVE MORE TO GAIN THAN LOSE

MY LIFE IS RICH WITH GOOD THINGS

I AM NOT AFRAID OF A STUMBLE IN THE ROAD

I
GLOW
WITH
OPPORTUNITY

VICTORY BELONGS TO ME

I AM
ABLE

I LIVE AS
IF MY
PRAYERS
HAVE
ALREADY
BEEN
ANSWERED

I
CHOOSE
FAITH
OVER
FEAR

MY
LIFE
IS
AWESOME

I
CONTROL
MY OWN
DESTINY

I AM
MADE
FOR
LOVE

I HAVE COME TOO FAR TO GO BACK NOW

I'VE GOT THIS

I HAVE THE POWER TO CREATE CHANGE

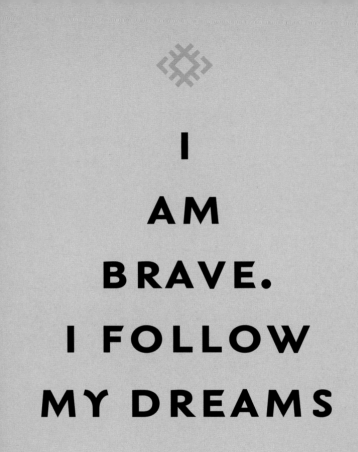

I
AM
BRAVE.
I FOLLOW
MY DREAMS